THE MAN WITH MANY PENS

Also by Jonathan Wells

Train Dance

As Editor:

Third Rail, The Poetry of Rock and Roll

THE MAN WITH MANY PENS

JONATHAN WELLS

Four Way Books
Tribeca

Please direct all inquiries to:
Editorial Office
Four Way Books
POB 535, Village Station
New York, NY 10014
www.fourwaybooks.com

Library of Congress Cataloging-in-Publication Data

Wells, Jonathan.
[Poems. Selections.]
The man with many pens / Jonathan Wells.
pages ; cm
ISBN 978-1-935536-63-5 (pbk. : alk. paper)
I. Title.
PS3623.E4695A6 2015
811'.6--dc23

2015006033

This book is manufactured in the United States of America and printed on acid-free paper.

Four Way Books is a not-for-profit literary press. We are grateful for the assistance
we receive from individual donors, public arts agencies, and private foundations.

NYSCA

This publication is made possible with public funds from the New York State Council on the Arts,
a state agency.

and from the Jerome Foundation.

[clmp]

We are a proud member of the Community of Literary Magazines and Presses.

Distributed by University Press of New England
One Court Street, Lebanon, NH 03766

CONTENTS

NO TICKET

His clothes are filled with tickets to past events
so he can hear the orchestra tuning up again
and the airplane landing near the diving cliffs

in Acapulco where the boys leap into the known
unknown in Speedo suits. All travel is continuous.
Time is ceaseless in his pockets. The piano recital

plays forever in its aftermath, its tides of notes
surging and retreating according to a lunar mood
for which the children have no table. The matinee

is screened over and over in the balcony
of his thought, specifically the part where the hero
realizes he's been pursuing her and is being

pursued in turn as they reach the precipice
of no regret. And then the fiery night calls
out to them and says no ticket will be needed.

WHERE YOU LIVE

Imagine you are coming home. Your front
steps are scattered with fresh petals or no
they are not there and you return in your
regular shoes from your regular leather chair.
The feeling is the same. The petals are just
as fine, the colors just as blithe and were placed
or unplaced by the same loving hand
or troubled hand or loving troubled hands.

You walk into the foyer and kiss her cheek
or the air that was merely there when she left
the room. Your kiss is just as eager or as meek,
your lips just as ready to speak as yesterday.
The difference is immense and thin.
The difference is the house you're living in.

THE BACKWARDS CALENDAR

Scrolling back, the days are not finished. Our children
are unlived, unborn, ethereal, concealed. We are

unmarried, unmet in our vintage gypsy clothing:
high-waisted pants, padded shoulders and fedoras.

The pen is not a chalice yet just dripping stains
of ink although I am already quiet, tucked in my

covers reading until the sheet melts into the lamp.
The silence is still sweet, sweeter than its rapture.

My mother and father huddle in their childhoods
in the cornfields and the Heights, a montage of

loneliness, before their collision in the city.
Their parents wait for them on the top stair.

Houses are barely furnished, the steps unswept,
metal chairs on the patio still plumped with snow.

Their high schools are vacant, teachers waiting
for their students high stepping through the drifts.

The blackboards are pure black, the chalk
isn't touched. Lessons are not learned, knowledge

is ungathered like seeds wind-spilled across the furrows
from a farmer's cupping hand. My grandfather

is standing by his storefront. His horse is unbridled,
the cart not fully loaded yet with eggs

and butter for the back doors. The photographs
fade out, the ancestors turning spectral, floating

uncaptioned in other families and countries.
Time is unassembled in the air, in space.

The gods still shake with their wrath of meaning
but the messengers are late, their language crude,

unequal to its mission. The curtains will never block
all the rays around the window. The wind begins

a song that the oak leaves will not finish.

OF SILENCE

I drove into the West:
its rock ledges
and slipper canyons.
The beautiful unwanted
spaces.

On that frontier,
the silence tended
a garden of stones
that I looked after
with my gardener's hands
that knew what would grow there:
the native rock and boulders—
that I loved for you
and kept for you
all of you
who didn't ask.

It was a silence of refusal
and freedom from refusal.
A magpie that swooped
and perched,
one silence inside,
others that stirred
the random sand,
the distance blurred,

the god-blown arches
that staggered and
released them.
Those we shared.

Now I keep heading west
into the hum of the sun.
Over a hundred miles to go
without a signal.

ABSENCE

The old oak leaf was blown away months ago
but the pavement still keeps its imprint,
an image of the October storm I remember.
I remember the flam of raindrops tapping
on the window like a tom-tom and the buildings
bunched together in the near dark,
magnified by water.

Our conversation was about absence the way
all conversation is about absence, what passed
without us, what never happened, what
we imagined in that emptiness.

You said I loved my secrets most, more than
anyone as if that was what nourished me.
You said cherishing them was what fortified
me and they were my deeper partners.

As you spoke I understood what frightened you:
the absence in my presence, the vacancies spreading
through me. I imagined the movement you hoped for
although I watched it pass without me. In this film
I moved toward you and embraced you as if all
and none of it were true.

INTERLUDE: THE ORANGE TREES

"The water left on their hands the memory of a great happiness."
George Seferis

Remember the feast we had near the ruins
of Gournia, the oranges shimmering like coins
in their leaves? The sails of a regatta across
the bay were breathless and cool as water.
The dreams we tasted again were the only
food we needed.

I loved the orange marmalade that was left
on your lips, the bitter pips, the copper
in your hair, the copper of the love we made
that was forged in our battle of earth and ore.
You who were malleable and metal.

The turrets outside town were as steady
for us as the moon's escort, as free as strays
stupefied under our café tables at night,
as free as pink oleander flowering
at the bottom of that gorge.

We were lucky those rare days to remember
that we didn't need to shake the branches
to gather our fruit and the race from buoy
to buoy into the wind, sails disappearing
beyond the curvature of water, wasn't a test
of our forgetfulness.

FOUR SHOES IN ONE

The shoes of struggle and resignation.
The shoes of oblivion.
The shoes of sleep.
These are the ones I was wearing
when I was lifted to the loft
of chanting doves and these are
the shoes that walked me home,
eroded soles dying of friction,
the scuffed up leather toes.
The shoes of rescue.
The shoes of mourning.
Here are the great gestures
and the hidden moments
lost within themselves.
Those are the soft shoes
I wore when I tiptoed away
from the wading pools of silence,
the laces tied so quietly.
The shoes of patience.
The shoes that spoke.
Here are the pilgrim's sandals
copped by roots and chiseled
by blades of stone along
the path of memorial
benches and crosses.
Here are the pilgrim's feet.

THE CONSTABLES:
SALISBURY CATHEDRAL FROM THE MEADOWS

In the fourth year of her afterlife
the day is confused and humid,
the evening limpid on his forehead.
She turns to him leaf by leaf to say
I will always paint this pasture
and falls piecemeal into the stream.

A rainbow resurrects her name
across the fields where a bullock sways,
woozy from its burden. Three horses
drag an empty cart through the shallows.
A dog watches the circling water
with no other mistress to follow.

The cathedral is weightless in the mind
as if it came whole not made,
no roots to anchor its composure,
but it rose from those shoulders and folds
inside the rain as it had once unfolded
inside us. A fan of Oriental wonder.

In the hotel of his heart some guests
stay forever but there are vacancies
to praise: a cornfield that was naked,
the calf that strayed into the forest,
forms the wind took in the ash trees
when she left them for the storm.

BEING AND NOT BEING

I was no one;

Water looked
through me

Cows grazed
my sweet grass.

The wind
lifted my
arms as if

they were
the flags
of no nation.

Then I was each one;
the calf,
the pond,

the breeze,
the banners.

SQUIRREL WATCHING

The leash is taut, her doleful eyes
transfixed as she lifts her snout to heaven,

every imagined taste almost in her mouth:
tickling tail boa, little bones, and haunch.

The squirrel freezes, his body spread-eagled
on the bark, terrified alert, condescending

to a love that smells so much like blood.
Each feature is profound: wide black eyes

stunned open, mini paws circling an acorn
in a blur, a dash of rust splashed on his back,

peaky ears and a white throat scarf.
Her love is the devouring of the whole

in parts. She waits measuring his speed
against her strike and leaps believing

it was true but if it were the world would
be purged of squirrels that looked away.

HANDMADE COFFIN

for Emmett Wallace

The harbor tide returned his things,
an unmailed check, spare license plate,
an old man's birthday cap as though
it was his freckled hand that placed
them in mine for keeping.

Which face guided him that accidental evening
with the winter moon to watch? Was it
the scowling one who always knew best,
whose wisdom he was trying to guess,
or the beguiling one whose smile seduced
him down the icy ramp?

Or was he just wrong footed.

The son planed his tears and sweat
back into the wood, a coffin made
of random parts, handrails cut from banisters,
the underside from ceiling patch.
It was big enough for all his parts,
(twisted leg, uneven shoulder, wristwatch,
fingerprinted glasses)
and let the soul thaw from contact
with his carpenter's hands and sap.
It fit him as well as his thinking chin
filled the notch between his thumb
and index finger.

THE FUTURE IS YOUR FRIEND

In the morning the afternoon says
I will wait for you and when you finish
we'll walk across the streets that rise
like the streets of the afterlife, streets
of air cantilevered through the clouds,
until we reach the river. We'll toss coins
into the water and count the bottle caps
imagining a perfect number.

The evening before you opens the front door.
Take off your shoes she says. Leave
your overcoat on the sofa. As you enter
she's asked the cat to prance across
the piano keys like an ecstatic on black
and white embers. He practices the shock
of sound because he can't listen to the music.
The notes splinter in a waterfall by Bartok.

The night stands its vigil outside your window.
Fresh mint tea, he asks. Biscuits from Scotland?
He knows you take your dinner eggs hard-boiled
still warm from the hen house. The light motes
of some stars will be sprinkled across your table
from a satchel he's always carried.

We owe everything we have
to those who can make us happy.

A TEMPORARY SEPARATION

After I left home and came back
to the uneven stairs my son
asked if we could go to the park.
We carried the football to the river

and threw it lazily back and forth.
Some throws traveled in a spiral haloed
by the sun and others end over end,
the laces ripped from our fingertips.

The distance between us grew and shrank
according to the weight our arms felt
or what we could reach with our human
strength across the vacant space.

THE MAN WITH MANY PENS

With one he wrote a number so beautiful
it lasted forever in the legends of numbers. With another

he described the martyrs' feet as they marched
past the weeping stones and cypresses, watched

by their fathers. He used one as a silver wand to lift
a trout from its spawning bed to more fruitful waters

and set it back down, its mouth facing upstream.
He wrote Time has no other river but this one in us,

no other use but this turn in us from mountain lakes
of late desires to confusions passed through

with every gate open. Let's not say he didn't take us
with him in the long current of his letters, his calligraphy

and craft, moving from port to port, his hand stopping
near his heart, the hand that smudged and graced the page,

asking, asking, his fingers a beggar's lucent black,
for the word that gave each of us away.

LOVE'S BODY

Love gives all its reasons
as if they were terms for peace.
Love is this but not that
that but not this.
Love as it always was.

But there is no peace in the mountain
cleft where the fruit bats scatter
from the light.
There is no peace in the hollow
when heat snuffs night's blue candle.

The outline of brown leaves
on the beach is the wind's body.

A crow is squawking at the sun
and the screech itself is dawn.
Let me hear every perfect note.
How I loved that jasper morning.

OTHER CAGES

The black gloss building mirrors
the upper town with its golden tower
and faint mauve clouds. The buses
on the avenue chew through the street,

their numbers written on their roofs
for the clouds to read. Below, a pipe bangs
inside the floor as if a man were trapped
somewhere in electrical coiling, tapping

a message in Morse code that said,
Save me now. Another citizen of the city
is misplaced in a crawl space, with a corner
of crenelated daylight the size of a stamp.

The flag unfurls in front of my post office,
a signal to the brave to come release me,
I'm ready. Against the wrinkled stripes
a graffiti of geese is scribbling south.

A canary saves his most beautiful song
for himself to make his cage invisible.
Because you cannot see my cage
I sing to tell you that it's here.

HIS NEXT CHILD

In the forest I walk first
so I can play the native's part.
The verses trail behind me,
a story of farewell.
I walk toward the scented leaves,
air like mead, sapling bark as sweet.
Each step is a garment I shed
as if I had wandered off
a pilgrim ship and lost my self,
stitch by stitch, in the maiden hills
where I was changed by a god
into his next child.

HOUSE OF WIGS

The sky was low. His head was a vase
of sorrows he wanted to fill with blossoms.
He stepped into the House of Wigs.
The saleslady said, "Try this one on. It's called
the *Mind of Fire*. It turns ashes into flame.
Prometheus was wearing it, they say, when
he was punished by the Gods for his compassion
and he barely felt the eagle's claws landing
on his stomach."

"This one is known as the *Parable of Spring*
for its rhythm and its pageant. The fresh
grass and forsythia will carry you toward
summer, your body lithe and unencumbered,
your hunger fed by fields of daisies."

"I'm wearing *Love's Crown*," she said,
"because love shouldn't be a neon idol
shining on a shelf. It must be worn
and worn through and not just the love
you bring but the love you can accept,
especially when the days are short
and brooding. Go ahead," she said.
"Put it on. Stand next to the light."

HART CRANE AND THE SEA FLOOR

The bells of the sea rang for him, so
he abandoned ship without his shoes to go
where he wouldn't be foolish to him-
self—escape the usual post love scrum,
scraped knuckles of the Cuban sailors with
rum-soaked tongues, sleepwalking dogs, myth
of the Bay of Veracruz whirring in his head.
What dialogues of men were lovingly misread
in the surf of voices rising and commingling
as he plumbed the waves, the nights' ringing.

On the sand floor sea hands pulled the rope
unbraided in the current, absent from the slope.
Chains of light, absolute noon, human shell—
but that was the angelus not the curfew bell.

THE ECHO POEMS

I. ECHO

White as x-ray bone she rises
sublime through the trees in stone
as if she knew what this grace was
and she was only nine, framed
between her errands and her games.
Her nymph's body surges underground
not knowing what this buried love is for.

Beneath her chin neighbors play Frisbee
on the grass and strangers take her
photograph. The final sun pours
into her sealed eyes and mouth
a saint of radiant stillness
who says this marble flesh is a prison
stone yet the mind flies
with the confetti of birds,
soaring into the vows of summer.
Silence succumbs to air and the blossoms
float down, the clocktower's fretted hands
notched against her ribs.

Questions flood her blood
and darkness, flee, and then she's gone,

taken from our vanquished arms.
She still speaks in the autumn leaves,
in the furrowed bark, in the singsong
of the children's swings.

II. NARCISSUS WANDERING

From town to town he carried
        his own sheets and towels
    like dressings for a wound
only he could see.
                In one pocket
he kept a book of common praise
           in the other an apple
and a camping knife. He knew
      how cruel neglect could be
in the younger mind and what
that hunger was like in the afternoon
             especially in a place
without a bank or grocery store.

The girl who loved him
          was only a child
having another tantrum. Her calling
haunted him from lake to lake.
           What refreshment
could he bring, what meal to share?
       With his fingers he'd comb
her fallen hair if only she'd stay quiet.

The air clotted and there was thunder
    like an amateur moving furniture
across an upstairs room before the rain
        began to smear

his face. Rarely was a sign
this clear in the water's overlapping lines.
                He left with his valise
and walking stick, the bones of his feet
burning in his mocassins step by step.
                The pond, her lips, these flowers
on the bank would not dissolve his name.

III. ECHO GONE

She plays peekaboo in the scumbled leaves,
in the arabesques of branches. She is absent

from the dawn, the treetops, the spiral pathways.
She hovers over me like a hologram and I reach

toward her when the light is tilted
until her image reappears. She is quicksilver

I fence in the thatch of my fingers that
falls away as I search her shuttered eyes.

She chances through me on a whim of wind
and particle matter, in stop-and-go traffic,

in open-air leisure, like the lover the cat
catches, fleeing, on both sides of his eyes.

She is my angel of stealth hiding in the upper
pasture not a girl repeating a playground rhyme

until her parched tongue collapses on the clouds'
soft palate. Her quickening shadow leaves me

panting behind her, cement-footed, as if I was
the one who was made of stone who could

only love what was made of stone.

DISSOCIATIVE

Once the body leaves the mind and knows
it is alone, it puts on its patchwork boots
and pale blue shirt with pink flamingos

to shop the streets until it finds another body
outside the mind for company. It can be
seized by whatever glows having lost

its inner guide: a firefly lady in a square,
a thin-haired man behind a still white
curtain standing next to a kerosene lamp,

or a field where a choir of boys warm
their voices in the moonlight before
the night's rehearsal. The body stalls

there, held by those searching notes.
Then the body that wandered out
prays it will fit back into its cradle.

PURPLE BLUE

My father said the earth
was purple blue
so I looked for it in the last lit hill
and the late clouds hanging over the ocean
like eggplants and plums.

I found it in the heart's flatted scales
and the scimitar arc of birds over
the estuary. I found it in the rain
relenting, a minor seventh chord.

I found it in you when you were subdued
your eyes flooded and distrustful of the water
and in rays of heat your hand messaged
into me when it hovered above my stomach.

I found it in myself
in the beauty of the ice and the bruise
of my stars widening and the calluses
on my fingertips from pressing too hard
on the guitar's thinner strings.

And I noticed it in him as he left us,
in the stained hollow of his cheek
in the shadow of his limbs
my sister washed as if he'd been a saint.
And in his face, a candle flame,
arrogant and wise, o first lord of light.

LE TRAPEZE

It is Tuesday. The Trapeze Club is closed.
The swingers stay home tonight crocheting madly
with their previously chosen partners. Above us
the stratocumuli pile up like egg whites
in a pan, ornately, the most rococo of clouds.

On the beat around our block that I parade
nightly, it is the monotony I like, the apparent
sameness of the pavement. My work is to spot
new cracks in the slabs lit by the available moon.
They hunt the evanescence of their scents.

Two Japanese girls passing by take me for a joy-
ride on the frolic of their English. My features
amuse them. I am the gerund of their evening,
a modifier not a verb. The dogs are impatient.
Love slows down the pendulum of our labors.

TINKER

He taps the glass and teases the swifts
through the mist with his fingertip
but it closes over them. The sun he tucks
inside the curtain hem. The clouds he calls
back from their shade in other countries.

He fixes her portrait inside the picture frame
and rearranges the hair on her bright shoulder.
He adjusts her chin and she stares back at him
through the leafy paint. Her eyes are dim,
her mouth is softening. He lets that love jump
back into his chest.

He tinks upon his rusted frame. The screws
rattle in their sockets, the thread twisting
against the plates of tin. He bangs his legs
with a tiny mallet. On his lonesome arm
he plinks a tune as if it were their song.
He sets aside his tools and waits
in the inner dark.

Seamstress of the fine nerves of the morning,
suture them with your needle and vanishing thread.
Isolate the wound. Direct the pinpoint beam.
Tell the story as you go of how they were separated
twice, once by time and once by thought,
and found themselves again. Let the stitches
melt into their magnificent cool skin.

THE UNEXPECTED ONE

What if you were the unexpected one
not made by the usual hands
who came into the poor man's room
bringing cooking oil and candlelight.
What passage would you gain
if you soothed his anxious heart,
what wings could you provide?

Would you judge him
by his sandals or his robe.
Would you weigh his palm
against your brow or measure
the canyons of his breath.
Would you tell him your stories
of the purple above the mountains,
the desert caves and gullies,
the scorpions and snakes.

And if this were his only life
would you tell him whether
the smell of earth after the rain
which swells inside his chest
would be enough to let him rest?

SIX-ARMED MUSICIAN

The six-armed man had six hands and a fretboard
of fingers for his chordings. He hosted six harmonies
inside him that rang out on the silk strings of his lute.

At the burgundy hour of evening he drank
six cups before the children lifted him to sleep
on the palanquin of their laughter.

Six willows cushioned him. Six wives watched him
pluck out his silver hairs and fetched him back
from the gyrations of his sleeping. When he awoke

to the menace of the night, six mirrors reflected
the dreams of his disappearance that six candles
beamed to the crows' nests that darkened them

in the mantles of their wings. Six lives were
unrepentant in his songs. Six cautious feet crept
along the bridge suspended over the chasm.

Six loves he cherished in the tunnels of his heart.
Six urgencies of praise he hid beneath his pillows.
Six worlds he conjured to grow old in.

PHANTOM SEA

The swallows tattooed on my chest
flew away as thousands of nautical miles
unspooled out of me. I followed them
for a while among stacks of bricks
before they faded away.
It was a flawless day in the time
when beauty still had its steeple.

On the cobblestones my legs buckled
with the waves. My clothes rolled
to the almighty chop and rigging sway,
the rank gulls upwind squatting
on the guardrails. The lower shelf of clouds
unscrolled along the horizon like hieroglyphs
for the captain to decipher.

The concubine napping in my rental bed,
her gold toenails glinting like lures
beneath the sheets, raised her head
and said with her Egyptian eyes,
I am your ocean now. The salt
will take care of the sea.

PREPOSITIONAL LOVE POEM

I wrote these words
for you, to you,
on you, in you,
beneath you, with you,
inside you, against you.

I wrote within me,
from me, toward you.
I hunted the words
between your open fingers
and your palm, listening
at your pale wrist.

After you'd gone quiet
I spoke the syllables
to myself to catch
traces of your voice.

DEER RUN

After two cycles of the moon, the deer are still
standing in the rapids. Their ankles split the river
into twelve new streams. A flash of danger in the water
and their leap to the bank is muted by damp leaves.
Their hooves make no sound and their white tails
leave no color in the dusk.

We watched them through the upstairs window,
the heat behind us as warm as the kitchen below
was ample, canned food in the pantry stacked
like ammunition and fruit in a rounded pyramid
on the counter waiting for the children's reach.

The deer fixed the river in the evening and a TV
sparkled in the corner after we found our dinner.
We were reverent and special then like guests
at a vision a god had offered that carried us
spellbound and cradled us in our ground.

FOR THE STRAYS

Tonight the world slips a notch on its belt
of trouble: the door isn't a door, the window
doesn't open. The howling on our block
is for anyone who'll listen. So come inside,
my dear, for a saucer of milk, a carpet bed.

I speak to you as I speak to myself
when I am missing, in a different shape,
a shadow puppet projected on a sheet,
with stringy arms and legs, a shapeless head,
leaning into the flashlight beam
believing it is the tunnel home.

Centuries I spent unborn, not sweeping
red and yellow rivers of leaves, twin-headed
dragons of time, along the pavement
or opening the door for ghosts tapping
on the glass. I practiced my absence
with a knife paring it back and back
until my silence was pure, pure enough
to drink.

A louder wind yanks us back
to these front steps, the scent of milk,
the phantom warmth, the neighbor's fanfare,
the sycamores anchoring our street,
the roots more powerful than chains.

ON MY WAY TO SOMEWHERE ELSE

At first it was coiled beneath me
then it was taken from my skin. Words
tricked it from my ears and mouth or they
tumbled from the air. Or there were arrows
to point me or the arrows were plucked out
or there was no grid or ladder to guide me.
I was pinned down. I let myself up. I wanted
nothing but to be told and told.
No one followed.

It found me curled on the roots
of a cut leaf maple my mother left me.
It came across me where I was hiding
or in my dreams where there was no exit.
It found me in my room without a map,
with the random shapes of chairs
and tables. It found me alone or in a crowd
or with a quiet hand across my neck.

It fell seamless or shanked. It was smooth
and sharp, smashed, or with missing pieces.
It was what was shed when the river
left its skin in the maple leaves,
the sheath I picked up
when I wandered out one morning.

TRAIL OF WORDS

Above the mortal
voices of the town
yeses and nos
your own petitions
there is a path
your feet take.

The higher you go
no one talks
and no one listens
except for those
you cannot see
and they hear
every breath.

Each step unties
you from time
until you are
one of the berries
on the juniper bush
the broader sky
the promontory rock.

The descent is also
the heel of your hand
rubbing against the weave
of paper moving down
a column of words
you are sculpting
now that you can
hear yourself again.

HOW TO LIVE NEAR A VOLCANO

If you could choose your place
it would probably not be here
where the trees will not leaf,
the earth is charred, the river
a gurgling red. Here the heat
peels the paint from your face,
your eyebrows are singed,
your tongue a boat that ran aground.

You can love the sulphur
and the smoke, the raw caldera.
You can love the scientists
who watch through binoculars
or you can love nothing.

You can be kind if you are kind
or careful with your movements.
You can offer banana or coconut
or you can offer nothing.

Wait. Listen. Is there a rumble
in the ground. Is that a tremblor
underfoot? Is the sky stained,
the sun bloated?

Hide inside you the choking
ashes. Hoard the albatross of
patience, the eruptions that are
contagious. Ask who would
choose to live in such a place.
Ask again.

Make yourself a monster to rise
against it. A coward to appease it.
Indict it, absolve it. Go further
inward. Go far away. Stand still.
Stay exactly as you are.

SETTINGS FOR THE END OF SUMMER

Someone is missing. Where is her full white face?
Which moon hides in the summer of her hair?
The days are as short as they were in the late
Edo period, the afternoons shutting down early,
maple leaves idle above the riddle of the garden.
The monk is humbled by the darkness of his ink.

Or the days are as long as when the Vikings
dragged the long haired women back from
the capitals they'd sacked and the shamans
foretold a breakage of the trees as if one wind
could plunder a forest or all the wildflowers
were suddenly scythed from the meadow.
The large stones with their wombs of grace
would miscarry too to show the spirit could
be hacked from almost anything.

And on this wan evening, nothing captured,
nothing awed, my fingers worry the rope
of longing that leads past my self, past
my father, to an ancient bell that told me,
the knell a hunger lurking in my blood,
to go people the earth with men like me
and unlike me. That is why the night
is numerous and deep.

GOOD NIGHT

The woman in my dream went home
to her children, books and lilies
which stained my fingertips and cheek
the color of sepia or rust.
Her leaving pierced the window
and flashed through me like sunlight
through an unfinished building.

I folded the towels and rinsed lipstick
from the rim. The faucet dripped
an easy rhythm to fall into.
In the water I was water;
its wings and hips and dancer's toe.
Her footsteps echoed away from me
as she climbed from room
to room.

Filled with fantasy and scrap
my head grew so heavy my arm
slept first. My metal fingers
drifted toward her who'd slept
beside me until the final frame.

THE FORGIVENESS ORCHARD

Concentrate on her hand and its freshness,
the loin of its palm, the apple-scented fingers
summoning back the slap that spread across
your cheek, gathering it in their seams of heat
the way a magnet drags the metal shavings back
that had once been part of it.
Don't ask questions
the hand can't answer. Focus on its form.

Let the hand that stung restore you
to the maiden grass you started from, a believer
again in the eidetic apple beyond your reach.

Relaunch the immortal humming of the bees
and let the sound swarm over you. Rewind
the stem. Put the apple back on the tree.

NOTES FOR YOUR DEPARTURE

for Kathleen Murphy

Keep walking in a circle so there will always be circles.
Hold the cashmere to your cheek so there will be touch
and saliva in your mouth so there will be moisture
and murmuring and ululation so there will be words
and word sounds and a half language of still wanting.
Gather the prayer rice scattered at your feet, each grain
a last offering of love. Circle your withered arms around
your sides and kiss your son. Your husband will ride
with you as he was always riding with you.
Pack and pack again. Leave the painting of the forest
behind with us for safekeeping.
Sweep the tulip petals purple in your hand.
Fix and refix your black felt hat. Run your fingers
round the brim and stand in front of the doorway mirror.
Remember yourself as you are now. Ready for departure.

THE MERMAID ON WEST TWENTY-FIFTH STREET

In the window of the vintage clothing store
she bathes upside down in the slatted sun,
her scales melting into a golden fin, her tresses

in a wreath around her human arms
that brace her neck. How I wanted
to bring her back to my landlocked room

and the sea too with its fans and currents,
nets of the fishermen drifting to the waves'
rhythm. To be human, she says, is to hover

above the street, to fill your lungs with air
and to dive back down through tiers
of water. To be human is to sink again

and be winched up believing this time
the world is borderless and safe.
She whispers this in the late powdery

light and then the street turns fair
and still. I know she knows what human
is because she's only part way there.

AN ARMENIAN WINEMAKER IN THE COPPER AGE

His sandals were found
pointing south from the cave
next to his drinking cup. The vines
he'd staked tailed into the ravine
where the river was sinewy
over the rocks.
Pooled water saved his quicksilver face
for the occasional sun to radiate.

Harvest by harvest he'd watched himself
perish in his son's dark eyes. If only
the sun would right that gaze
and make it light like the wine
in his mouth, as playful
as his childhood name.

At dusk, father and son stood side by side
without glancing sideways and both wondered
why all of the blackbirds gathered
in the same flowering tree
and how they could agree
on which one was the sweetest.

LITTLE EASTER ISLAND HEADS

Near mine, their eyes do not defend
the shore or scorn the red plague tide.

These bedside gods shape the transom breeze
around their heads from outer air. I touch

their pumice crowns for luck like rabbits' feet
the druggist sold us for a quarter. Between

the blinds at 4 a.m., the oasis hour, I search
for signs of my blue water that should be there,

the tree within the tree that will lead me
back, its silence ringing. I lean into what

I cannot hear—the cast iron sea shattered
on the reef, long distance gulls calling

out across the hours. These tabletop gods
watch my chest rise and sink. They guess

the games of seeds and knives, chutes
and cries that shout inside my head

that they must protect with their local powers.
We are small but not diminished, not calved

from some larger stone. We crouch together
and share this night, the stars that pierce,

scorpion and archer spelled out beyond our scale,
the moon that casts its blades of light.

SONG OF THE SIX-ARMED MUSICIAN

His song is made of hands. One points
playfully to heaven. Another pauses

above the strings waiting for its chord
to strike. The violent one thrashes

the spruce top. The gentle one holds
its palm over the sound hole. The echoes

wash against its lines. Some are too quick
to see. The musician, an imp, bows

his head in false blessing. Is he too agile
to fall, too light-fingered to love?

Each hand is pure but the player
himself is unsure beneath his pose

that any song or key or costume or skin
is strong enough to keep the notes together.

THE MAN WITH

With one he fucked
the Holy Ass of Baal

and wouldn't stop while
its parents watched. From another

he tied a boat made of balsa wood
that bobbed on the foaming sea.

One frothed all by itself.
He wrote Sap has no other Grail

but this one in us, no other path
but this slow dripping one

down his monkey chest.
Through his spasms and his shakes,

his ink and craft he took us
with him asking, asking each

one of us to pull him off.

UNEXPECTED GUEST

The house doesn't know I'm home.
The table lamp praises the open book
for the promise of what's to come.
Our clothes were left where they were
or we left them as we'd been.
A rhombus of sunlight opens
the wall like a balcony window.
The rafters make an intermittent sound
of Jew's harp and banjo wire.
The sofa lowing, the skylight whistling
a roofless tune, the ceiling fan paddles
the air like a snarebrush circling a drum.

The house summons me home.
It wants my footsteps tipping the grass
silver on one side as I approach it,
my fingerprints on the doorknob,
my breath fogging the front window.
It wants its brother, its partner
in time, its morning mirror.
And I was singing as I entered
not knowing I'd been so loved.

THE WINTER OF ONE GLOVE

Was it for me the somersault from her pocket
the day the wind shooed winter away?
Was that hand's nest my next assignment,
my Monday morning bounty served
on a blanched platter, the breakfast
of my New Year's banquet?

Four leather fingers bowing to the thumb.
Red cashmere genuflecting at the wrist, a gesture
wasted on the pavement. A yardman's creased
mitt open-fisted on a post like an owl's glower.

How many hands would fit inside each one
like Cinderella's foot in Cinderella's slipper.
Was my slab hand the key inside the lock?
One lock to pick, an empty glove to answer.

TWO CURRENTS

A white egret threaded some branches
dangling over the river and floated down
to a dry mossed rock in the parachute
of its wings, their span closing over
its fragile slate-flat body. Through
a lace of spring leaves the other sky
was innocent of thunder and the grass
was as ripe as sun.

There is more to love than the day
and its recitals. There's the kiss ruined
on the roof of my mouth, lips
that regret their meaning
and will not heal by morning
and the heart itself sinking to the bottom
of its cage, a prisoner of its bone-white
imperfection.

What I told the wind was blown back
on me like chaff. I swallowed my kiss
and my tongue was pinned inside my
throat. The egret with a heart like mine
stood at the bend between two rivers,
two currents splitting its desparate claws.

SMOKE SIGNALS

At dinner, the crystal candlestick suddenly smokes
black. The blue flame flickers but doesn't blow out.
She lifts her white hand toward me so quickly
that I cannot tell if it's the one her heart sent
to thread my hair or the prudent one that knew
she'd already traveled too far for her safety.

The smoke that fumes inside you, fumarole,
is not the smoke that coils above your head,
is not the smoke that pours from the tower's
body, furnace, separate from its source. It is

the smoke of the day that burns down in you
like a fuse and explodes in cobalt to the sky's
limits. Sunk in each others' arms, we watch
the glowing. Even the smithereens are blue.

POEM WITHOUT WORDS

The falling leaves do not make a poem
unless they fall through you, from you.

The brittle edges rasp against your chin.
The sea is silent in their ribs, no rows

of trees along the beach. A poem without
words or sound. Three smokestacks press

toward you through the haze. You know
they're there to help you up.

THE SECOND BOOK OF LOVE

He read aloud to her from
the second book of love.
And all the other books.
She listened without listening
as if it were a mist that
drifted through her. He read
not noticing she slept.

He didn't know these words
would one day move his lips,
the old feelings would slip
away and disappear.
The trees would shine in an amber light
that the once-fresh light turned into.
Some pages would be as bright
as flarings on the sun. Others
would be torn and torched
under a magnifying glass
without remorse.
Crossed-out words could
still be glimpsed.

It was a work that circled,
a story that lay open
on the lectern of vacant rooms
and jumbled nights

written by an unlikely pair of hands.
It was made from the five senses
and the sense of hovering
above the air.

It was the book of hours,
the strip of days.
In its lines
was the confusion
between what was unsayable
and what couldn't be said.

SUMMER EVENING WITH THE WINDOWS OPEN

A muted trumpet is playing
a standard in the park, a flourish
the tulip leaves soak up. Walkways
of fog link the spaces between
the trunks while the melody snakes
into our loft around the thunder.

The sky calls for me with phosphorus.
My leaving lasts for hours in the afterlight
but I stay seated at the table. The wine
hints at fruit in orchards I can't imagine.
My exit is forever, a figment of the night.

Maybe tomorrow you will be my usher,
escort me down the hall to my departure,
lead me to the outside wall and we'll watch
the shadows grow oblong on the grass,
my accomplice, my company, my friend.

DRESS CIRCLE

To drink the sun directly
from the tap he sat by the window
in his leather chair barechested
and patient. The hummingbirds
teetered on their invisible threads
watching how his throat worked the gold.

It was a late afternoon's a cappella light
that soaked through him like yellow dye
through silk. There was enough for every soul
although lines reached around the block.

The sky, scarcely blue, graced the stage
from its rooftop perch and a thousand
amphitheater eyes were glued
to his next gulp. The rain had whetted
every appetite for opera.

He drank as if it were the last performance
of the sun. The other ticketholders stumbled
across the street littered with ticket stubs.
The garbagemen with brooms were swept
into their shadows but he swore
he could still taste that twilight on his lips.

NOTES

"The Constables: Salisbury Cathedral from the Meadows" refers to the 1831 version of the painting.

"The Echo Poems" were occasioned by Jaume Plensa's sculpture titled *Echo* which was displayed in Madison Square Park in New York, New York, in 2011. It stood forty-four feet tall and was modeled on a nine-year-old girl who lived in his Barcelona neighborhood.

"Six-Armed Musician" and "Song of the Six-Armed Musician" refer to the cover painting by Christopher Wood, British painter, 1901-1930.

ACKNOWLEDGMENTS

Thanks to the editors of the following publications in which these poems appeared: Academy of American Poets Poem-a-Day, *AGNI, Ellipsis, The New Yorker, Paris Review* Daily, *Ploughshares*, and *Whiskey Island.*

Thanks to those who read these poems and helped make them better: Jane Wells, Robert Pinsky, Erin Belieu, Christopher Merrill, and Martha Rhodes.

This book is dedicated to Gabriel, Delilah, Juliet and Alexander Wells for keeping the world fresh.

Thanks to Ryan Murphy, Martha Rhodes and Four Way Books for their attention to every aspect of this book.

Jonathan Wells's poems have appeared in *The New Yorker,* *Ploughshares, AGNI,* The Academy of American Poets Poem-a-Day program and many other journals. His first collection *Train Dance* was published by Four Way Books in 2011. He is a co-editor of the Tebot Bach New World Translation Series with Christopher Merrill and lives in New York.